Perry Como's Christmas Cracker

a play by Stan's Cafe

ISBN 978-1-913185-08-4

Published by Stan's Cafe
Birmingham, UK
2020

www.stanscafe.co.uk

Perry Como's Christmas Cracker © Stan's Cafe 1991
Photos © James Yarker 1991
Publication © Stan's Cafe 2020

Contents:

Perry Como's Christmas Cracker   1

Bonus Material
Original Programme Notes   38
Perry Como Brought Into The Fold   39
Touring Perry Como Dec 91 - Jan 92   41

Perry Como's Christmas Cracker

Introduction:

The actors are always playing Bob, Bill or Mary. On most occasions this character will in turn be playing one of the pantomime figures. The text which follows covers action taking place on the stage, there are also some guidelines for the shape that improvised backstage dialogue should take. The backstage dialogues should be used to develop the relationship between Bob, Bill and Mary. The most important thing to remember is to have fun with it.

Characters:

Bob plays Gabriel and Herod
Bill plays Innkeeper and Prince
Mary plays Mary and (reluctantly) Hamlet the dog who in turn (reluctantly) plays a reindeer.

Set and Props:

A small stage is set up within the theatre's own stage.

A white screen up-stage conceals props and costumes. Down stage right and left are narrow flats painted as stage curtains signifying wings. A clothes line crosses the screen in a loop, head and chest high, this is used to move items of set across the stage. The sets are just hardboard board signifiers, simple images boldly painted – house, fireplace, tree, sun etc. A number of these have their own integral battery powered lights.

Props are made in the same style as the set - wooden, bold and flat.

Costumes:

Bill and Bob wear D.J.s and bow ties. The character costumes could be just hats, full costumes or Tommy Cooper style costumes split vertically half and half. Mary wears a duffle coat.

Prologue:

The house lights are up, wing space is lit. Casiotone music plays.

Mary is in the audience, she evidently is not of the audience. From backstage the voices of Bob and Bill are heard, their text is improvised around the following points:

Show time is approaching, Perry has to be called. Bill is ready and returns from a fictitious backstage space to say the star has not arrived. There is anxiety yet they decide that they can perform the show themselves.

Bob moves centre stage holding a wooden microphone, he addresses the audience.

Bob: Good Evening ladies and gentlemen, boys and girls. Uh... I'm sorry for the delay. We are having a bit of a problem, a small little problem, in fact more of a hitch than a problem. There's been a slight hitch. Mr Perry Como is unable to make it tonight... that is, he is feeling sick and dizzy and his tongue has gone blue and his dance troupe aren't well either. Yes, we are all very disappointed that Mr. C cannot be with us but don't worry, the show will go on. Their parts, all their parts will be taken by myself and my good friend Bill.

[Bill enters to meet his audience, Bob keeps control of the microphone]

Bill: Hello.

Bob: Great, great, that's lovely. Right.

Bill: There is just one other thing you forgot to mention Bob.

Bob: Oh, what's that Bill?

Bill: Well, there is one part that neither of us can play.

Bob: Yes that's right Bill. There is one part that we need some help with.

Bill: So we were wondering, is there anyone in the audience tonight who would like to come up on stage and help us with the show? Anyone in the house called Mary?

[Mary squirms, looks around and then puts up her hand]

Bob: Lovely, lovely. Mary come on down, come up here love. A big hand for Mary ladies and gentlemen. Right Mary love what's your name?

Bill: I think we already know that Bob.

Bob: Oh yes of course. Where are you from Mary?

Mary: [Quietly, giggling and embarrassed] London.

Bob: [Offering her the microphone again] Sorry what was that? I think you're going to have to speak up a bit.

Mary: London.

Bob: [As if London is a really unfashionable place] How lovely for you. No, really, well someone has to live there I suppose. Right and what do you do Mary?

Mary: I'm a nurse.

Bob: Really! Ladies and Gentlemen don't the nurses do a tremendous job? You must have hilarious stories about that.

Mary: Well no, not really.

Bob: Ha ha. Marvellous. Right if you'll go off with Bill he'll help you into your costume. Mary, ladies and gentlemen. Marvellous, what a character.

Once again sorry for the delay but I'm sure the absence of Perry Como will not spoil your enjoyment of "Perry Como's Christmas Cracker". Thank you.

[Exit Bob. The Casiotone music starts and lights fade as before. This time the show begins]

Scene 1:

[A house comes on with clouds and two trees. Lights come on in the windows of the house, smoke comes from the chimney and a fairy with a light in her wand flies on. Tacky pastoral music plays with Christmas radio adverts beneath.

With a laugh and shriek, Gabriel stumbles onto stage. She is the pantomime dame. Rearranging her dress she sees the audience and does a huge double take. Canned laughter almost helps Bob out as his routine dies its inevitable death]

Gabriel: Hello! I didn't see you there! Well this is a nice surprise. Where have you all come from? [Pretends to listen to the audience] Devizes really!
I once knew a man from Devizes
Whose assets were of different sizes,
The left was so small it was no use at all,
The right so big it won prizes.

Anywhere else? Weston super Mare? That's near Devizes isn't it!

Right. Hello - someone sniggered. Careful Sir you might wake the others. Honestly, I've seen more life in Stirling Albion's centre forward than you lot. Oh I hear we've got some Albion fans in tonight sorry boys!

No, it's great to be here... well to be honest it's a relief to be here. At one point I thought we'd never make it, honestly, we went round the centre of town five times trying to find this place. Honestly the person who drew our street map was useless. I couldn't understand any of the street names. Still it's great to be here in Warsaw.

We found the place eventually, well obviously you know that, because here I am. Anyway I don't know why we bothered to be honest, you should see the dressing rooms, hell holes, not fit for royalty let alone actors! Well yes I am exaggerating, they do have hot and cold running water... running down the walls. And they're so small, honestly, this big with a curtain instead of a door, hardly room for us all to get in.

My name's Gabriel, some say I'm an angel, some just take advantage. You've been an audience, thank you good night.

[Bob exits but Bill in the wings reminds him that was an old Jimmy Tarbuck routine and not part of the pantomime. Gabriel re-enters as before]

Gabriel: I'm the angel Gabriel. I'm from up North, from Chorley. I'm one of Chorley's Angels. Well anyway I'm Mary's Fairy Godmother and I have to protect her from the evil and horrible, spotty, fatty, pooy breath and smelly bot scoundrel King Herod. Can you do me a favour? If you see him give him a boo. You'll recognise him because he is so undesirable. In fact he is everything that I am not.

Now I've got to rush back to Mary, she's been doing the housework.

[A scene change brings on a fireplace and Mary carrying her script]

Gabriel: Here she is. Hello Mary.

[Mary is very embarrassed and lost for words. Gabriel continues the script taking her lines for her as well]

Gabriel: I saw Herod today.
Would you like to know what he was doing?
He was having both his nostrils pierced and linking them with a little chain.
You'd like to know why wouldn't you?
To stop his nose running!

I knew you'd like that one. So what have you been doing today?
Have you been practising our Christmas song and dance routine? You'd like to do it now?
Oh all right then lets do it right here!

[Bill comes on stage to join in the dance but Bob pushes him back off instructing him to "do the sticks". The song and dance routine is led by Bob with Mary trying to learn and follow the steps, she is well behind, the dance is poor. Bob is glad to be the centre of attention. There is a solo section in which Bob does some tap dancing. He attempts ever more extravagant moves with Bill adding tapping sounds with sticks from the wings. Bob then goes for some speed tapping encouraging Bill to tap faster and faster, there is the inevitable fall and the dance is finished prematurely]

Gabriel: That was wonderful Mary. One day if you keep practising you could be like Ginger Rogers.

Mary: Thank you Auntie you were good as well. You could be like Roy Castle.

Gabriel: Why thank you charming girl. Time to stuff the turkey. Off we go. Bye kids!

[Off stage Bob is anxious as to whether anyone saw his fall. Bill reassures him and changes the scene to Herod's Castle. Bob claims the part of Herod and Mary is asked to provide the thunderclap]

Scene 2:

Herod: Greetings oh miserable minions! I am Herod, King of Everywhere. No doubt you've heard of me? No! Well I'm a sort of evil Genghis Kahn. And you must be my subjects. English I expect, no my mistake, Natural History. What is this a train-spotters convention. Well I hope your Bic pens leak, your pencil leads break and your anoraks are permanently leaking.

[To others off] Make haste you crawling worms! You sluggards! Bah! You are slower than a slug with blisters.

Mary staggers on as a golf caddy. Innkeeper is with her, the rest of the scene takes place with Innkeeper and Herod playing golf]

Mary: Mutters Complaints.
[She realises she's read out a stage direction]
Oh, this bag is heavy!

Gabriel: You smell of a million sewage systems! One more complaint from you and I'll turn you into a frog! Then you'll hop it. Laugh frog! Your master has been witty.

Mary: [Laughs]

Inn: Very drool your effluentness!

Herod: I don't know why I bother with you two, the Krays would have been more use, come to think of it Tom and Jerry would be more use.

Inn: We are trying boss.

Herod: Yes, very trying. I've got enough problems without looking for your balls in the rough, now try and stick to the fairway.

Inn: He sounds like my probation officer.

Mary: Ooh [grabs her nose].

Herod: What is it now?

Mary: I think it's going to be a bogey.

Herod: What!

Inn: Sorry your roughness, she's a bit green.

Mary: [Inspecting her finger triumphantly] It's a double bogey!

Herod: Putt it away. As I was saying I've got enough problems without you clowns.

Inn: What is it boss?

Herod: Oh nothing that you'd understand.

Inn: Fair enough.

Herod: Well if you persist in asking. The truth is that I, Herod, am in love.

[The others laugh. In the next speech Bob makes an attempt at a Frankie Howerd impersonation, Bill gives him some subtle pointers]

Herod: What are you laughing at you mangy pack of hyenas? I'm in love with the sweet and lovely Mary, so stop your sniggering and titter ye not, for anyone caught laughing at me I shall turn you into a golf tee, stuff you in the ground and strike balls off you with my two iron. Understand?

Inn: Yes your Barbara Cartlandness. Are you going to ask her out to a club?

Herod: No, you are.

Inn: But wouldn't you be jealous?

Herod: No, for you shall ask her out for me.

Inn: But what if she doesn't fancy you?

Herod: I am Herod, the handsome, wise, powerful, witty, intelligent King of Everywhere, why wouldn't she 'fancy' me?

Inn: Well...

Herod: Bring her to me!

[The two minions run off but Herod calls the Innkeeper back with the flag so that he can get another imaginary hole in one. Off stage in helping Bob change costumes Mary accidentally rips one of them forcing them to be worn half Gabriel on the right Herod on the left]

Scene 3:

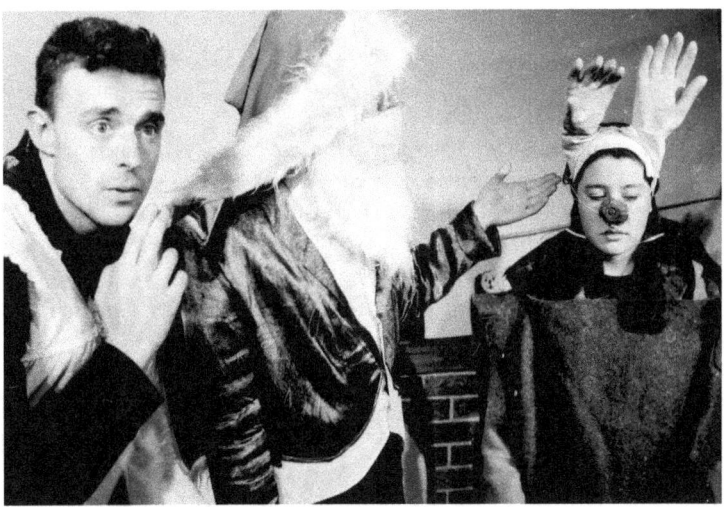

[Gabriel arrives back from the shopping]

Gabriel   Oh dear what a palaver, oh lovely, what a pullover. I've been out buying presents for the relations. I hate it, the shops are so crowded and the relations are a funny lot. Do you want to hear what I got in the end? Right then for my Grandad (what are you laughing at, I'm not that old you know) my Grandad's bald so I got him a toothless comb, my Dad's getting a cigarette lighter, it doesn't work but that's all right cos he's given up, my Mum's getting a pair of bloomers [flowers pulled from bag] and for my sister I got this plate [half] well she's only my half sister.

> The only problem is Mary; I could get her a mountain bike, or a Nintendo, or a computer, or a Lego battleship. She's a good niece she deserves the Earth and oceans. So I think I'll get her some compost and a bottle of Perrier. Oh Girls listen, just imagine if you could bottle Perry Eh!

[Prince enters dressed with a beard and Santa hat]

Prince: [Coughs] Excuse me.

[Gabriel is greatly surprised and falls over. She stands adjusting her clothes]

Gabriel: Oh dear I've disarranged me duvet. Do you mind mate you nearly crushed me curly kale, I bet I've got percussion now. I'll 'ave you.. oh eh don't I know you from somewhere? The telly? Don't tell me, you're Santa!

Prince: Hello good lady and Merry Christmas to you. I am Santa and this, is my trusty reindeer, Rudolph.

[Mary is eventually persuaded on stage wearing a pathetic reindeer outfit and an attempt at an Arabian Headdress]

Gabriel: Why is Rudolph wearing a dishcloth on his head?

Prince: Because he thinks he's Rudolph the Red Nosed Valenteno.

Gabriel: Sorry I asked, anyway Rudolf, I mean Santa, what can I do for you? Have you brought me my pressie early? That's brilliant, how did you get Michael Aspel in the sack? [Aside] Well there's no harm asking!

Prince: Well I cannot tell a lie, I'm not really Father Christmas. I am a prince from a far off land and this isn't really a reindeer, it's my dog. [Mary takes off dishcloth and red nose].

Gabriel: Really, what sort?

Prince: It's a Great Dane.

Gabriel: I don't know about that but it's certainly a big dog.

Prince: I was sent away by my father the Sultan because I refused to marry of the local princesses. He says until I have a wife and riches I shall never return to his land. So here I am, looking for a wife and a fortune.

Gabriel: Well darn my socks and bless my blisters, who'd have thought. Well go on whip your whiskers off. I've never seen a real live prince before!

[Prince takes off his hat and beard]

Gabriel: Cor knock me knees and heave me bosom ain't 'e 'ansom? It's... he looks just like - Perry Como!

Prince: [Bill delighted to be able to address his audience launches into panto rubbish]
Hello I'm The Prince, you must be [local town].
Hello [local town] Let's do this properly.
Hello [local town] That's better!

Gabriel: Oh this is marvellous. My name's Auntie Gabriel, let's go to the Eskimo's Arms and have a couple of snow-balls to celebrate.

Prince: I'm sorry, I don't think I could afford that.

Gabriel: I know a restaurant where we can eat dirt cheap.

Prince: Who wants to eat dirt! No, I'm sorry Auntie Gabriel, it was lovely meeting you but I've got to go to Herod's palace to make my fortune, could you direct me?

Gabriel: Oh dear, you should have stayed to meet my niece Mary, she's lovely, a nice niece. Herod's palace is a long way, you go into the desert and it's right after the four thousandth

	sand dune. Then left at the second mirage and fourth oasis on the right. Won't you stay for a cup of tea?
Prince:	No, I'll return when I have my fortune but I'm worried about taking Hamlet through the desert.
Gabriel:	Hamlet?
Prince:	Yes, he's the Prince of Great Danes.
Gabriel:	Right, well you can leave him here, we'll look after him won't we kids?
Prince:	Thank you so much. Good bye. Merry Christmas. [Exits]
Gabriel:	Merry Christmas! Cor, what a stocking filler, a real cracker! Come on Hamlet. Let's find Mary. [Both Exit]

Scene 4:

[Mary still holding her script, concentrating really hard, walks slowly through the forest of Christmas trees which cross the stage, a sun goes in the opposite direction, when this has disappeared it is replaced by the moon and the Christmas trees, which are passed around the back of the stage to reappear, now have lights lit up on them. Mary is frightened by the dark and sings a TV advert to keep her spirits up. The tune is from Away In A Manger.]

Mary	"I like to eat Baked Beans at Christ-i-mass time, They are festive and red and they make me feel fine. I only like Heinz beans, no others will do. I give them to Santa, it's the least I can do".
	Oh dear, I should be the happiest girl in the whole wide world. I've got a lovely Fairy Godmother who looks after me and we live in cheerful honest poverty together, but it feels like there is something missing from my life, something that.. oh, I cannot explain.

[The Prince enters and halts suddenly at the sight of Mary]

Prince: Cor, what a smasher! She must be Mary, Auntie Gabriel's nice niece.

Mary: Oh! Could it be that he is the something missing from my life?

Prince: Hello, I'm the prince from a faraway land, you must be Mary.

Mary: Not only are you handsome prince, but you are very wise, how did you know I was called Mary?

Prince: Partly because your fame and beauty is legendary throughout the civilised world and beyond, even as far as [local town] and partly because your label's sticking out.

Mary: You are a handsome prince and a wise man, are you rich as well?

Prince: Unfortunately no, for otherwise I would ask you to marry me this instant oh pure and sweet Mary. I am off to Herod's palace to make my fortune but then I will return to take your hand.

[There is a beautiful song and dance number *A You're Adorable*. Bill leads Mary and is enjoying the dancing but she is actually being pushed around and manhandled, the dance is not very elegant. Growing confident and impudent and not impressed by Bill's attentions Mary adds her own unexpected letters to the end of the song. Bill improvises desperately]

Mary: Oh he's so romantic. Yes, yes good Prince I will await your return, please hurry back.

Prince: I will. [Exits complaining to Bob about Mary's behaviour]

Mary: I'm in love, wait until I tell Gabriel. [Exit]

Scene 5:

[Mary is supposed to be sweeping up but instead is sitting looking miserable. Gabriel enters in her night-gown, crossing the stage to go to bed]

Gabriel: Nighty night, sleepy tight, don't fill your socks with dynamite. Hold on, what's wrong Mary?

Mary: I'm in love with The Prince and he said he'd marry me but he won't, he'll meet someone nice at Herod's palace and never return.

Gabriel: Look, you shouldn't be canoodling with the royal icing, if the Sultan found out he'd have us decaffeinated.

Mary: Are you incinerating our family's rubbish?

Gabriel: No, I just don't like to see you upset, there are plenty more princes in the sea, you'll see. Like this one for instance [producing a tin of Princes tuna]. Now cheer up and whistle a happy tuna, after all, it is nearly Christmas! Nighty night.

> [To audience] You will look after her won't you? She's a bit upset about the dashing prince dashing off. Thanks, I know you will. Nighty night then. [Exit]

[The lights go down with Mary left on stage. She holds a beautiful dress up in front of her and does a few hesitant dance steps, she thinks she is Cinderella. The Innkeeper leers at her]

Inn: [To audience] At last I've arrived in Nazareth where Mary lives. This must be her.

> Good evening, my name is Mr. Innkeeper. I keep an inn in the beautiful resort of Bethlehem and you have been chosen as the special winner of a free luxury holiday there. So, if you would like to come with me.

[There is an unnatural pause and Mary starts deviating from the script]

Mary: You are an Innkeeper in Bethlehem?

Inn: [Having to improvise] That's right and you are the lovely, sweet, pure and chaste Mary who hasn't got a boyfriend aren't you?

Mary: Maybe.

Inn: Try this slipper on. Yes it fits. You're Mary all right. Do you want to marry the wicked horrible tormentor and sadist, the gruesome ugly and evil Herod, King of Everywhere?

Mary: No thank you.

Inn: Ok, well you're coming with me anyway.

Mary: No I'm not.

[Bill seeks help from Bob in the wings. Mary looks through her script suspiciously. Bob says that Bill is being incompetent and pushes him back on. Inspired, Bill gets carried away in an elaborate mime full of cliché which ends in Mary being tied up and dragged off. Bob points out that she has not moved. Bill is forced back onstage panicking he freezes and the blurts out]

Bob: Some poetry:
In the depths of the night
Twixt the sheets and the black
I feel your curse fall upon me
It strangles and pummels
and wakes me screaming 'Mother'.
Thank you.

[Bob is furious, Bill summons fresh resolve]

Inn: Right, you're coming with me to Herod's deep dark dungeon of blackness and stinking torture, where you'll be married and live in blissful harmony for the rest of your days. [Mary has already left]

Scene 6:

[Morning. Prince comes looking for Mary. In trauma after the last scene Bill delivers his text functionally]

Prince: Mary, Mary, where can she be? Hello everyone. I've come back to see Mary but she seems to have disappeared. Talking of disappearing. [Exit Bill]

[Enter Gabriel with a banana in her ear]

Gabriel: Mary, Mary. Oh hello everyone. Have you been here all the time? And you haven't even popped out for an ice cream? Then you can tell me where Mary's gone?

Pardon. I can't here you I've got something in my year. Oh I feel a ripe banana. That's better, now what was that? She's been taken by the Innkeeper to marry King Herod! But you were supposed to look after her. Why didn't you stop him?

You can't trust anyone nowadays! Oh dear oh dear. Mary's been taken to a life of riches, holidays and servants and cream cakes and I'm stuck here. What am I going to do? Bo ho Bo ho. [Bill has entered]. Oh it's the Prince, what are you doing here?

Prince: [confused] I've come to give Mary her Christmas present. But oh my goodness, you're right I'd never thought of that, we've got to rescue Mary at once. Where's Hamlet?

Gabriel: Why is he a tracker dog? [set up for a gag].

[Bob senses things are going out of control, he forges on, not waiting for the audience responses and does 'subtle' gesticulations to Mary in the wings who is refusing to come on as Hamlet]

Gabriel: Let's call him. Hamlet. He didn't hear us, come on kids you can help. Hamlet! Tell you what Princey you stay here and call and I'll go and look for him.

[Bob goes off to find Mary. We see him running frantically around backstage. Bill is still doing pantomime standards with the audience. Eventually, looking slightly desperate, Bob says he's found the dog. He emerges just holding the dog costume in his hand]

Prince: [Getting enthusiastic too early]
Let me go to Baghdad to rescue The Princess, um Mary. We'll seek Mary out, we won't return without her. You stay here madam this is no job for a woman, adieu my love!

Gabriel: Not on your belly Nelly.

Prince: Right, but if you're coming you must promise me one thing.

Gabriel: What?

Prince: Hold on tight.

Gabriel: I hope you know what you're doing.

Prince: Hamlet... Fetch.

[They have worked out a pantomime slapstick exit]

Scene 7:

[Off stage there is a whispered argument. Bob is briefing Bill and Mary about the next scene. He outlines what should happen. He urges Bill to stick to the script and get straight on and off. He patronises Mary and says she's doing very well. Bill enters as the Innkeeper with Mary pulled along behind]

Inn: Come along Mary. I'm taking you to the castle of not very nice, but soon to be your husband King Herod. And you'd better not give me any trouble or it will be the worse for you. You hear me?

[Mary stops walking Bill has to start improvising]

Inn: Why have you stopped? Get up you lazy dog. There are still hundreds of miles of desolate desert to cover before sunrise.

How dare you interfere with my incantations.

You deliverer of free newspapers, you player of excessively loud car stereos, you... horrible person!

Come on, move!

[Bill is getting wide eyed and desperate in his improvisations and without knowing it Mary rescues him from silence by starting her own story]

Mary: We've travelled hundreds of miles over the desert and I'm so tired. I can't go on like this, something is very wrong, terribly wrong.

Bill [Seizes on this cue and tries to use it to get Mary off stage with improvised text]

Mary: I've got this feeling, I think I'm going to have a baby. I'm a pregnant woman. I need to be carried on a donkey.

	I want a donkey.
Inn:	A donkey, umm a donkey.
Mary:	I'm not going anywhere without a donkey because I am going to give birth to a baby. I am carrying a precious burden, the ultra-sonic scans say it's a boy and they say his name shalt be called The Baby Jesus. My time has nearly come and we must make haste. [Assigning Bill the role of Joseph] Joey, don't just stand there, help me.

[Mary pretends there is a donkey, and then makes Bob pretend to lead the donkey and her off stage]

Mary: Ssssh, that's all right, ssh, quiet now. It's all right little donkey. I know it's a dusty road but there's not far to go. Come on Joey take my hand please to steady me on my way down this pitted and rutted path.

Look, look Joey, that little twinkly village of lights down below us. It must be the tinsel village of Bethlehem. Let's hurry Joey, I think I can feel the contractions coming on.

[Exit together]

Scene 8:

[During this scene Mary looks for an opportunity to perform the next section of her play. A lamp post moves across the stage in the burning desert, Prince crosses in the opposite direction]

Prince: Come on Auntie Gabriel, nearly there.

[Prince exits Gabriel enters mopping her brow]

Gabriel: Phew it's 'ot 'ear. We've been travellin' all day in the burnin' bakin' 'eat with nothing to eat except sandwiches. What do you call a small dead pig? Hamlet. Come on

Hammy. Oh would you believe it, he's found a lamppost in the middle of the desert. Still that's convenient night comes on quick out here.

[Snap to blackout. Gabriel pulls out a torch]

Gabriel: Told you. I'd better go back and find that tragic hound.

[The street light comes back on. This time it is illuminated]

Gabriel: Hamlet, Hamlet, wherefore art thou Hamlet
[under his breath] Bill, Bill
Alas poor Hamlet. I knew him well but now he's gone and left.
Bill, do the dog!
A dog, a dog, my kingdom for a dog.

[Bill furious and mortified enters wearing the dog's ears and nose. He stands centre stage while Gabriel does a pantomime routine running around, trying to find him. Eventually Bob does a huge double take at seeing Bill in costume and almost bursts out laughing]

Gabriel: Now listen kids, if you see 'im give me a shout. Shout "Auntie Gabriel" as loud as you can. Will you do that? Good! Where is he? Which way did he go? This way. Right! Don't forget to shout kids. Oh you lot are 'opeless! You're just messin' me about! It's not fair. Oh where is he? Where are you? Oh no he's not [etc.]

Oh there you are. What's up? You think Mary's this way? But we're going this way. All right Lassy, lead the way. Princy will just 'ave to make do on is own won't 'e kids. Right! [Both exit]

[Between scenes 8 & 9 Mary ventures onto the empty stage to play out the next section of her nativity play. Bill and Bob are arguing backstage]

Mary: We've arrived. It is the night time outside the inn in Bethlehem.

>Look little donkey, at last an inn. It sounds a bit rough but it is cheap. I will see if they have a garage because they probably don't like donkeys in the rooms. Wait here little donkey and don't take sugar from strangers.

>Now I'm going into the Guest House. Inside it is gloomy and...

[Bob is sorting out the scenery, putting Herod's castle on stage]

Mary: Oh. This must be the Innkeeper putting up his decorations. When he comes over I shall ask if he has a room for me and my baby.

[Bob starts his scene and hisses at Mary to get off stage]

Mary: Oh, they're full. [Exit]

Scene 9

[Innkeeper is supposed to phone Herod to tell him that Mary is safe but Bill starts to get his revenge. Bob does not understand the stage convention of him and Bill both having telephones on stage so he makes the Innkeeper answer the phone]

Herod: [to audience] Greetings my little camel droppings. How are you liking it here in the desert? Too hot? Too dry? Can't wait for the interval? Tough! Ha Ha. That desert rat The Innkeeper is dune to phone about now with a progress report. "Dune" get it? A beaux jest!

>Ah I can't wait for my lovely wife to be delivered. I've brought a lovely dress for her and bunches of flowers, besides, my Cape Of Evil needs ironing and there are piles of washing up waiting for her here in Castle Herod. Mmm what can I do whilst I wait? I could knock on

people's doors and run away, or set off car alarms, or rattle sticks down railings. No, I know, I'll make horrid faces out of the window to frighten the little children.

[The Innkeeper enters making the sound of a telephone ringing, he puts Bob's down for him and positions himself on the opposite side of the stage]

Herod: The phone! Innkeeper answer the phone.

[Bill indicates he can't because he is the one ringing. Eventually however he realises he's going to have to play along walking from phone to phone]

Innkeeper: Herr Baron King Herod the Great and Mighty Evilness of Everywhere's residence.
Hello. May I speak to King Herod please?
Right. It's for you.

Herod: Who is it?

Inn: Who is it?
It's me, the Innkeeper.
I'll just tell him.
It's the Innkeeper.

Herod: Well don't just stand there, give me the phone!
There's no one there!

Inn: Hello is that the mighty evil, spotty, horrid, pooy breath scoundrel King Herod?

Herod: Yes.

Inn: This is The Innkeeper.

Herod: Yes I know, I know!

Inn: I've got the girl.

Herod: Good man, good man. Where is she? Where are you? Is everything all right?

Inn: Well, there is a bit of a problem.

Herod: What! What's happened?

Inn: Well, she says she's pregnant.

Herod: What! Pre pre pregnant how.. who.. when?

Inn: She says it just happened and it wasn't anyone. It's going to be born on Christmas Day and it's going to be called The Baby Jesus, so there.

[Bob is stunned, he is desperately thinking on his feet and the following speech is half him and half Herod]

Herod: She can't have a baby, she can't.. it's not right. She's going to be my wife, what will people say? She's done it on purpose. Oh I'm angry, so angry! Wait till I get my hands on her! I'm so angry I'm.. I'm going to kill every little baby everywhere so she won't have a baby when I marry her then people won't laugh at me.

Inn: There's something else.

Herod: What?

Inn: I've hidden her and you can't have her unless you give me a thousand pounds.

Herod: What?

Inn: You can't have her unless...

Herod: I heard you! What, are you crazy? I'll kill you!

Inn: No you won't.

Herod: Give me one good reason why I shouldn't.

Inn: Because I'm hundreds of miles away, on the telephone.

Herod: Well, when I find you, I'm going to kill you!

Inn: Okay, um Good-bye.

Herod: Yes, Good-bye.

[Bill whizzes off stage]

Herod: Right. I'm going to find them and when I do there'll be trouble. Now, where's my car?

Scene 10

[Just as Scene 9 ends Mary enters. Bob is just exiting, he double takes as he passes her but decides to let it pass. She fulfils a useful function for Bob as he tries to regroup off stage and instil some discipline into Bill.

Mary arrives without acting and sits down centre stage. She thinks for a moment and then starts talking]

Mary: This is a sort of shelter. There are wooden bits up there. This is straw on the floor. There's a door I suppose, over there and a window, only it's really dirty and so you can't see through it. And there are all sorts of wild animals lying around, only they are all calm and peaceful and friendly with each other.

What's happened is that there were no rooms in the guest house inn and now we are here and I've given birth to The Baby Jesus.

[She takes off her duffle coat and makes it into a baby]

and I'm now holding The Baby Jesus and trying to keep him quiet.

Hush now, don't cry.. oh and Joseph has gone out, to buy some chips.

Hush now, don't cry The Baby Jesus and I will tell you the story of how you came to be born.

It was a long time ago and once upon a time when I was doing the washing up. There was a shiny light like lights in the rain and there was a voice like a radio voice played really quiet but really near and it was The Angel, come from the clouds.

[Looks round to Bill who is pushed on stage by Bob]

Mary: And he stood near me and I was frightened. "Who are you?" I say and the Angel points at me and says "do not be afraid because I am an Angel and would never beat you up. You are going to have a baby and you've got to call it The Baby Jesus".

Inn: I'm the Innkeeper. This is the cellar bellow my inn, escape is impossible. No one can hear you and you've only got mice to eat, until Herod comes with a thousand pounds to marry you. Good bye. [Exits]

Mary: Then the Angel leaves to play her harp.

[Bob has looked at Bill backstage and Mary on stage. He enters determined to sort Mary out but she immediately pulls him into her nativity too]

Mary: Ah Joey, I'm glad you're home. This Angel called round while you were out and said we are going to have a baby. It's bad luck I know but it means we must get married and go to Bethlehem on our honeymoon. Go and pack our bags please.

[Mary turns back to the audience and Bob, defeated, exits]

Mary: So that's what they did and she had the baby prematurely and here you are. Yes. [Unsure]

[Backstage there is a briefing]

Bob: Right we're going on, we're going to do The Prince and Herod scene and we are going to stick to the script, right? And if you deviate from it in anyway, I'll kill you, right?

[The Prince comes on and after a while Mary leaves]

Scene 11

Prince: Was ever a man so unfortunate as I? First I'm lost in a sandstorm. Then I lose my faithful hound and now I could really do with an ice-cream.

Isn't it deserted here.

I hope we find Herod soon. The thought of my lovely Mary in the hands of that terrible tyrant is driving me crazy.

Okay, look is that Herod's palace or another mirage up ahead? Could my journey at last be over?

Herod: Welcome to my secret palace in the sand. Once you have entered you will never escape. You will remain forever in my service for only by magic can anyone leave this shifting dune fortress. From now on this will be your home, oh too perfect Prince of Nowhere

Prince: [Aside] Oh I'm in so much hot water I feel like a tea bag. Thank you for your kind greetings your video nastiness. Unfortunately I must decline your offer of eternal slavery, for you have my beloved Mary. I have come to her rescue, lead me to her oh Disgusting One.

Herod: I shall do better than that, she is in prison awaiting our wedding you shall join her there to say your last good-byes.

[There is a rather appalling stage fight with lots of obvious trickery and collusion between the performers. The fight may include a rather cheap Star Wars spoof. Herod eventually comes out on top]

Herod: Right, you shall join my future bride in my dungeons.

[Herod frogmarches The Prince off stage where Bill reminds Bob that Mary is not in the dungeon. They enter and start improvising]

Herod: I suddenly recall she is not in my cellars, she has not yet been brought to me, no matter, I shall still throw you into the cellar.

Prince: If you do not have her who has her? For he who has her, I shall have him.

Herod: Not that it's any of your business, you son of a camel, but my trusty Innkeeper is bringing her to me.

Prince: Oh.

Herod: I shall tie you up here so that you can never escape. Then I shall go and find Mary myself.

Prince: Would it not be better if both of us were to search, for two heads are better than one, especially if one of them's yours, your Not Very Cleverness.

Herod: No. You shall stay. I shall search.

[Bob and Bill have been doing a good deal of unspoken communication. Bob has tied up Bill so he is out of the way as he tries to sort out the narrative mess. Bob exits. Bill improvises a light sabre and with this The Prince escapes]

Scene 12

Mary: The same place as before only this time I think it's wood shavings on the floor and rain is coming through the corrugated iron roof.

Little baby Jesus, now you are born and wrapped up in pampers and Mothercare kit, listen to a little bedtime story I think I remember from when I was a kid like you.

There was one day when in a little village, everyone had locked up their doors and shuttered up their shutters.

> They were all playing blind man's flirting and sinking loads of festive cheer because it was The Christmas Time when you must not drive your car at night.
>
> On the hills above the town were some shepherds. Shepherds? Well they are like farmers. There were some farmers on the hills and they were smoking fags when they were told that there was a big star coming to this little village so they went and checked it out.

[An apparently improvised chase begins with Bob as Herod trying to find Mary and shake Bill as Prince off his tail.

The chase involved a dune buggy with the speedo fixed, a secret passage through a cliff which is blown out, a climb up a rock face, swinging over a canyon, crossing a rickety bridge, falling into a torrential river, a speed boat, survival amongst sharks, water-skiing on crocodile backs and ejector seat in the speedboat puts Bob almost into orbit with Concorde heading for his stomach, the Cap Of Evil is used, Concorde crashes, a parachute is burnt apart and inflatable underpants cushion a landing in Mary's back garden.

Throughout it has been Bob and Bill improvising against each other. Eventually Bob performs as if Bill is Mary]

Herod: Mary at last I've found you, I've been through so much, now please say you'll love me.

Prince: Well actually I'm not Mary but [peels off imaginary mask] The Prince.

Herod: No you're Mary wearing a Prince mask wearing a Mary mask.

Prince: Prince.

Herod: Mary.

[Bob and Bill are screaming at each other until the fight becomes personal. They collapse on the floor exhausted. Mary includes this situation in her story. At different points Mary includes the actions of Bill and Bob in her story, even going so far as to pull them back on stage when they try to sneak off]

Mary: They came in through that door, all exhausted because of their journey full of adventure. They came through that door and said.

"Is this where the big star is staying tonight?"

and then I go

"yes, good farmer shepherds, he is here and is called The Baby Jesus."

[Bob apologises to Bill for his behaviour, there are mutual compliments and apologies and promises, then slowly and appallingly it occurs to them that they are still on stage in front of an audience they stand up wide eyed and silent]

Mary: Well when they saw The Baby Jesus, they had wide eyes and didn't know what to say. They thought they'd been fibbed to because they were looking for a big star like Perry Como but only found this mum and her kid in a smelly old shed with old gardening jumpers and mouldy pots in it.

They were all pissed off, what with the pubs being closed, it being Christmas and all. They whisper to themselves, "it's a rip off" and turn to go. Then I say:

"Wait good men. Don't go. This is The Baby Jesus and he has only just been born and you are the first people to come and visit. Please do not be angry for that would make him sad."

Well they looked at you and thought you were cute and might be a child protégé and so gave you lots of nice

Christmas presents, to keep.

Then the farmer shepherds had to get back to their sheep and left on a bus.

[Bill and Bob exit]

Mary: And so that's how it was that The Baby Jesus had his first visitors.
... and I think I've got it wrong again.

Scene 13

[Bob timidly approaches Mary to try and end the show]

Gabriel: Hello Mary, it's me, Gabriel.
I'm in your mind like a vision.

> Now that you are feeling frightened and want to be rescued. Remember when I gave you that star and said if you are ever in trouble throw it in the air and help will come.

Throw it now Mary, throw the star.

[Bob holds out a star ready for Mary to include in her text]

Mary: This is the back room in a pub and there are barrels there and crates there and the sound of Slade's "Merry Christmas Everyone" coming through the wall.

I remember how there was a bright light in the sky. It was bright in both the day and the night and people thought it was a U.F.O. but it wasn't, it was a star.

[Mary has taken hold of the star and at this point lets go. Bob and Bill follow the star together, slowly across the stage and it is eventually put on the clothes line resulting in a Wise Man style tableaux]

Mary: The star was there to show the Kings which roads to take on their camels. They followed it very carefully and stopped in motels and bed and breakfasts on the way and wherever they stopped they put their advent calendars up on the wall and every morning opened another window and scoffed the chocolate which was behind. And behind the last one was a silver chocolate star like that one and then they knew the next day would be Christmas and it was the last day they could buy presents before the shops shut so they went shopping and got Terry's All Gold and a Frankenstein game and er something. And they gave them to The Baby Jesus but he thought they were crap because the Kings hadn't read the ages on the side and they were too old for him to play with, but because he was good he said "thank you very much, they're just what I always wanted Uncle King and Uncle King and Uncle King."

... that's nearly right I think.

Scene 14

[Triumphantly Bob as Gabriel, hauls Bill on and off stage whizzing everyone through the rest of the plot]

Gabriel: Ah Princey I'm so glad I found you in the desert, look do you see that new star in the sky?

Prince: Yes.

Gabriel: Do you see how it's moving?

[There is a slight pause whilst Bob moves the star]

Prince: Yes.

Gabriel: That's the magic star I gave to Mary for when she needs help. If we follow it we will find her. Come on.

Prince: Right.

[Both exit]

Bob: [In the wings to Bill] Stay!

[Herod enters]

Herod: Ha ha a star. I shall follow it and find my future wife and kill everyone else. [Exit]

[Gabriel and The Prince enter]

Gabriel: Mary, thank goodness we found you in this stables. Quickly, you must run. Herod will soon be here. Look I have two tickets you can fly to Egypt, go!

Mary: But what about The Baby Jesus, he must come with Joey and me when we escape. We need three tickets.

Gabriel: Of course, ah I've just found a spare one, here you are now, go! Ah, it's too late, he's here!

Herod: So here you are, you pathetic people. I was going to marry Mary and I would have done it too if it hadn't been for you meddling kids. Now I'm going to kill you all with my magic.

Gabriel: Look out!

Herod: On this shower I use my magic power.
You shall not be wedded, instead you are now deaded.

Gabriel: His spells are useless. His wand is juiceless.
You are not dead, but alive instead.

Herod: By my darkest powers I command you.
Drop them in the poison stew.
That includes the hag.
Who I feel is dressed in drag.

Gabriel: Light will win the day.
And darkness go away.
Herod is good.
And will do what he always should…'ve.

Herod: Oh I feel quite dizzy, in fact I feel quite good.
Hello what a lovely couple. Good evening.
And my goodness who is this beauty who's hair is like golden threads in the Autumn Sun?

Gabriel: Didn't know I could do magic did you? He's quite dishy now he's not evil don't you think?

[Bob sings a duet of *What Kind Of Fool Am I?* with himself over a recording of Perry Como's version. In the end it is all too much, he breaks into sobs and Bill steps in to end the show]

Bill: So there we are. Everything turned out fine. Gabriel and

Herod are getting married. So are the Prince and Mary and The Innkeeper is giving them a free holiday in Egypt. Thank you for watching our pantomime. Goodnight.

[There is a theatrical end with bows and waves Bill and Bob exit and hug each other in the wings Mary has waited patiently and when the house lights come on she also finishes her story]

Mary: So baby Jesus, on with the story of the other baby Jesus as I remember it from my Grandmother and the old books.

Mary and Joey were very happy with the little baby Jesus because he never cried and had a shiny halo. They wanted Christmas to go on for ever. But Herod had sent the hit squad to get them in the dark. They had to run away even though it was a Bank Holiday and all the trains would be packed and they did.

And then.... well, the baby Jesus grows up to be a carpenter like his dad and...

I think that's the end.

Original Programme Notes

Stan's Cafe present for your entertainment

Perry Como's Christmas Cracker

By ditching Joseph, cutting the shepherds and making Gabriel the dame they created the perfect pantomime show-biz Christmas. They looked set to break the bank, but when the star of the show pulled out, they lost prestigious venues and had to perform it all themselves.

With no notion of how to entertain and no wish for art, three people take the stage. These are bankrupts who find that there is nothing much left to say to people who have heard the story better told many times before.

It theatre is a commodity, theirs are damaged goods. For Christmas without Perry is but a pale shadow of all we are told to love.

Bill	Mark Courtney
Mary	Sara Liney
Bob	Graeme Rose
Writing / Direction	James Yarker

[For some reason Richard Chew went uncredited for his work on the Casiotone providing much of the music. The programme also failed to note that a degree of devising went on in rehearsals and a degree of improvisation went on in performance. Audiences were left to assume, correctly, that all the sets, props and costumes were designed made or found by the company]

Perry Como Brought Into The Fold

The first show Graeme Rose and I made together having decided to form Stan's Cafe was a short piece for an evening of performances organised by The Centre For Gender Studies in Hull, but the programme for that event didn't have the company's name on it and I don't think it was very good, so we'll pretend that it never happened...

Perry Como's Christmas Cracker was Stan's Cafe's first show. It's not a very stylish show to have as your first show. For years I was a bit embarrassed by it and would occasionally pretend that our history started with the much more polished and sophisticated *Memoirs Of An Amnesiac*, which we made the following year. For years *Memoirs*, with its lush soundtrack, playful approach to time, layering of realities, interplay of humour, poetry and visual flair felt much more recognisably a Stan's Cafe show than the knock-about *Perry Como*. Then in 2010 we made *The Cardinals* and that show's use of 2D scenery, staged offstage performance, a marginalised but ultimately central female character, biblical vs secular narrative line and lo-fi approach to soundtrack were all recognisably from the *Perry Como's Christmas Cracker* world that any doubts about this show's place in the company's history have vanished. It's gone from 'awkward outlier' to 'seminal production' in a mere 19 years.

Perry Como's Christmas Cracker was an idea I brought with me to Stan's Cafe. I was (and still am) obsessed with the relationship between form and content. I'm interested in lining these two elements up so they work harmoniously together, but I am also interested in what happens in the tension when they don't align. *Perry Como* makes broad comic play of the damage done to a traditional nativity play if you stuff it into the pantomime form. At the same time it uses this tension between form and content to speak about the tension between our secular and religious celebrations of Christmas.

The show was incredibly rudimentary, we made it with next to no money. We paid for plywood props and petrol out of our earnings (I was washing up and Graeme had an admin job at the Employment Service). I suspect Graeme took the lead in prop painting and maybe I took the lead in costume sewing, either way we rehearsed in the front room of 85 Ombersley Road, the house we were renting at the time. Graeme's mate Richard Chew - from the Royal Academy Of Music and thus ludicrously over qualified - knocked out cheesy versions of known tunes on my terrible old Casio keyboard.

We recruited Sarah Liney, who had acted in shows I'd made at Lancaster University and Mark Reynolds, who Graeme knew from Birmingham, to be in the show with us. It must have been a profit share but it's difficult to imagine there being any profit.

Having read and digested scripts for a couple of standard pantomimes I sat and wrote *Perry Como's Christmas Cracker* (Graeme nominated Perry Como as the correct level of celebrity to not turn up). Once written the script was then amended in rehearsals working with the cast. Signifiant passages were left for improvisation and theatrical / physical 'business'.

It was rough and ready but full of energy and seemed to go down well. After a modest tour in 1991 the piece was revived for Christmas 1992 and a run at MAC in their tiny Hexagon space. For this I took over from Mark (possibly because Mark wasn't available but possibly because we were trying to save money). Where Mark as Bill was all suave charm I was all surly recalcitrance as another brother, Brian. We added a fake interval in which the audience were given custard creams. I don't recall what else changed between versions.

As well as setting Stan's Cafe on its way this show also provided one of our most memorable touring moments. I will leave this for Graeme to explain.

James Yarker, November 2019

Touring Perry Como's Christmas Cracker, Dec 91 - Jan 92

"It's only a paper moon, setting over a cardboard sea..." chimed Perry from the portable cassette player. "..If only you believed in me, when I believe in you?..."

Stan's first project was an abject exercise in the art of 'making do'. We weren't short on belief... just everything else.

In the absence of rehearsal premises, we laid out our poster-paint set in the front room of the rented terrace in Ombersley Road; In the absence of decent publicity material, James's Amstrad worked overtime to deliver copy to those precious venues who had booked the unheard-of Cafe; in the absence of a tour-van, Mark Reynolds's Volvo 340 was deemed suitable for the job (being the only vehicle we could get our hands on).

With four of us travelling in it we were faced with the dilemma, though. Should we slice all of our set into three foot sections to fit into the boot, or buy a roof-rack? The latter meant investment that we could scarcely afford but I'd seen a 'Paddy Hopkirk DeLuxe' roof-rack for sale in Halfords and felt certain that it was right way forward for the company. And so it seemed.

We were flushed with the initial success of shows at The Oval House, in Wokingham and Eastbourne. It was time to break into the Provinces. And so to the City of Bath we drove. The memory lingers like the taste of sick in your throat. What now seems like high comedy smelt at the time like raw fear. We were on the M27 near Eastleigh when a freakish gust of wind caught the hardboard panels of our set. I had taken a great pride in my fanciful square-lashings which bound rope across hardboard and onto Paddy Hopkirk's finest. Those lashings were immovable. So, the wind ripped the roof-rack clean off the Volvo's runners and away it went. We watched through the rear window as it took flight.

In that sickening moment it was not so much the evening's show on my mind as the imagined pile-up. A multi-vehicle horror carnage involving a crap set. I kept thinking...'we'll be in gaol for not being properly insured'.

We were approaching a Service Station so Mark pulled in and we ran back along the hard shoulder, looking for the accident.....the debris....some sign....anything.

But there was nothing. Save for a few splinters of wood whose source could not be verified there was absolutely nothing remaining.

Perhaps our set ended up underneath a juggernaut and got dragged along to a ferry port to be apprehended by Customs? Perhaps it disintegrated on impact and vaporised into the sweet Hampshire air. A Highways Patrol Car listened to our concerns and drove to the next junction and back to investigate. They couldn't find a thing, either.

The best we could do was drive to the next venue via a timber yard. We loaded up with a couple of panels of hardboard and some '2 by 1'. That afternoon we hastily built ourselves a set and by 7.30 the paint was dry and ready for animation.

The whereabouts of that first set, still clamped onto the Paddy Hopkirk roof-rack, remains a mystery. If ever found intact, it must have been the cause of certain interest.

Graeme Rose, July 2005

[Extracted from an essay about early touring originally published on the company website]

About the illustration and design

The illustrations for the covers of these books were undertaken by students at Birmingham City University as the final module of their first-year illustration course during the Spring/Summer of 2018. The images were developed through workshops using variations of the theatre-devising methods employed by Stan's Cafe but adapted and applied to the making of visual work. The resulting work was shown in the pop-up exhibition *The Something Of Somebody Something* at Stan's Cafe's venue @AE Harris in May 2018.

The design concept of the books was produced by final year Graphic Design student Aimee Chapman. These were then further developed for print in a collaborative process between Stan's Cafe and the University's Innovation Product Support Service (IPSS) which involved helping the company to select appropriate DTP software, undertaking training and selecting a suitable print on demand service.

Gareth Courage
Lecturer in Illustration
Birmingham City University

www.ingramcontent.com/pod-product-compliance
Lightning Source LLC
Chambersburg PA
CBHW071758080526
44588CB00013B/2287